BECOMING ME

FROM SURVIVAL TO SELF

A Guide for Women Ready to Rise

SHAWNTA AUSTON

DEDICATION

For every woman who has ever swallowed her truth, carried more than she should, apologized for needing rest, or dimmed her own light to keep someone else comfortable-

This book is for you.

And for my daughters, Ashley and Jada, who have shown me what becoming looks like in real time.

For my son, Justin, whose quiet strength carries a healing all its own.

For my granddaughter, Emiko, who is already becoming more than I ever imagined.

For every woman in my lineage who survived so I could rise-

I honor you.

I thank you.

And I am still becoming because of you.

EPIGRAPH

"Becoming isn't about finding yourself. It's about returning to the parts of you the world taught you to abandon."

TABLE OF CONTENTS

A FOREWORD TO THE WOMAN BECOMING

To the woman holding this book-
You didn't pick this up by coincidence. Something in you was ready.

Ready to tell the truth.
Ready to stop shrinking.
Ready to loosen the grip of survival.
Ready to rise into the woman you were always meant to be.

This book is not here to fix you-because you are not broken.
It is here to reveal you-the you buried under years of performing, pleasing, protecting, and persevering.

Move through these pages slowly. Let them speak to you.
Let them confront you.
Let them hold you with tenderness and clarity.

And when you reach the end, may you find yourself standing firmly at the center of your own life again-
soft, strong, rooted, whole… and becoming.

HOW TO USE THIS BOOK

This is not a book to rush through.

It is a book you experience.

Approach each chapter with honesty. Let each truth meet you where you are.

Sit with the reflection questions-they're not filler; they're the doorway to your own clarity.

Write freely, without editing or performing. This is where your real voice returns.

Honor whatever emotions rise; they are evidence of your unfolding.

Revisit The Becoming Truths whenever you feel old patterns creeping back-they're your anchors.

Let The Becoming Spaces be a sacred pause where insight can land and deepen.

Treat the activations as invitations, not assignments. They are here to support your evolution, not pressure it.

Allow each section to build gently on the last, creating a rhythm of awareness, honesty, and healing.

This book is meant to be lived-one revelation, one truth, one breath at a time.

A NOTE ON YOUR JOURNEY

There will be chapters in this book that feel like someone turned on the light in a room you've been avoiding.

Moments of truth.

Moments of grief.

Moments of holy recognition.

Moments of awakening you didn't know you were ready for.

Let every part of it come.

Let every part of it teach you.

Let every part of it escort you back home to yourself.

Because you deserve to meet and embrace the woman you are rising into.

And she has been waiting for you.

CHAPTER ONE

THE MASK I WORE -
AND THE GIRL I HID BEHIND IT

Power Statement

I didn't learn to silence myself by accident. I learned it because it kept me safe. The smile protected the peace. The silence protected me. And for years, I mistook that survival pattern for strength. I never realized the mask I wore would one day become the barrier I had to break to return to myself.

When Silence Costs You Yourself

You can pretend for so long that even you forget you're pretending. You can master the smile while your spirit strains under the performance. People will applaud your composure while you slowly disappear behind it.

That's the danger of silence: it doesn't just keep conflict out - it keeps *you* out. And before you know it, you're living a life you're not fully in.

How My Silence Learned to Speak For Me

My mask didn't arrive in one moment - it was built slowly, through tiny shames and unspoken rules. I learned early that "good girls" didn't challenge adults, didn't cry too loudly, and didn't disrupt the room. If something hurt, I held it. If something bothered me, I swallowed it.

Over time, I became exceptional at appearing unbothered. My smile hid what my voice never felt safe enough to say. My silence became a strategy. My composure became a kind of currency - people trusted it, even when it cost me pieces of myself.

I carried that pattern everywhere: school, friendships, relationships, motherhood, leadership. By the time I stepped into professional roles, I could perform pleasant compliance with Olympic-style precision. I agreed when everything in me resisted. I softened myself so others could stay comfortable.

There's a deep loneliness in being present while your voice is absent - a quiet ache you don't always recognize until you realize you've started losing yourself.

When My Body Told the Truth Before I Did

Every morning on my drive into my office in downtown Los Angeles, something in me felt heavier than the day before. Not tiredness - heaviness. A soul-deep exhaustion I couldn't stretch or sleep away.

One morning in the parking garage, I caught my reflection in the rearview mirror. My eyes looked dim, like someone had turned down the brightness. My smile looked practiced, not lived in.

And something inside me finally whispered the truth:

I wasn't just wearing the mask.

I had become it.

If I didn't reclaim my voice, the woman behind it might disappear entirely.

The First Crack in the Mask

My transformation didn't arrive with fanfare. It came quietly - the way most truths do.

I noticed when I said yes but meant no.

I noticed how my body tightened every time I swallowed what I needed to say.

I noticed the moments I stepped out of myself so someone else could stay comfortable.

The noticing was the beginning - the first tremble of truth waking up inside me.

Awareness is where becoming begins.

The Becoming Truth

My voice matters, even when it shakes.

My truth deserves space.

I will not shrink myself to keep the peace.

The Becoming Space

Sit gently with these questions:

When did I first learn to quiet myself to keep the peace?

Who taught me that their comfort mattered more than my truth?

What mask do I reach for when I feel unsure or unheard?

Where in my life do I feel muted?

If my voice spoke freely today, what would it say?

Let your truth rise without editing.

Your Turn to Rise

Choose one small moment this week to practice honesty in real time. It may sound like:

"Actually, that isn't what I prefer."

"I see it differently."

"No, thank you."

Small truths build brave lives.

Each honest moment strengthens the woman you are becoming.

Before You Turn the Page

You've seen the mask - now you'll see the cost. Silence always sends a bill, and the price of disappearing is far higher than you think.

Every becoming starts with a whisper, a tremble, a truth long buried beneath the performance of strength.

Turn the page.

The cost of silence is about to be revealed.

CHAPTER TWO

THE PRICE OF SILENCE AND THE WOMAN WHO FINALLY STOPPED PAYING IT

Power Statement

Silence always sends a bill. And the longer you avoid your truth, the heavier the cost becomes. Holding in what was meant to be spoken is never weightless - it leaves marks, even when no one else sees them.

When Silence Feels Like a Battle Scar

When you silence yourself to keep the peace, you don't avoid conflict - you relocate it. Every unspoken truth becomes a burden your body eventually has to carry. Every swallowed boundary becomes a bruise you learn to ignore until ignoring is no longer an option.

How I Learned to Disappear in Plain Sight

My silence wasn't dramatic. It was polite. Predictable. Easy to overlook.

At the Los Angeles law firm where I worked, my title said Firmwide Billing Manager, but what I really managed was everyone else's comfort.

The Director of Client Relations didn't oversee my department - but she acted as if she did. Her preferences became priorities. Her ideas became directives. Her voice filled the room even when the room wasn't hers to lead.

And me?

I smiled.

I nodded.

I made myself agreeable, even when something inside me tightened in protest.

One day made the cost impossible to deny.

A fire had damaged our old building, and after the attorneys and staff were displaced for a couple of months, we were transitioning to a new high-rise in the area. I was responsible for organizing the larger section of our office - equipment, workflow, seating, everything. It was a Saturday between my son's basketball games when I rushed downtown to finalize it.

The building was quiet, peaceful. I worked with intention, putting every desk and printer exactly where it made sense. She was there too, arranging her much smaller section. By evening, both areas were complete, and I drove home feeling competent, grounded, and proud.

Sunday morning, my phone buzzed.

She had a "new vision" - not for her area, but for mine. She wanted the entire layout changed to better suit her team.

She wasn't asking. She was instructing.

And the part that still makes me shake my head?

I said, "*Of course.*"

I said it automatically, as if the words belonged to someone else.

Then I drove back downtown and undid hours of thoughtful work.

On the outside, it looked like cooperation.

Inside, it felt like erasure.

That day, my silence stopped being invisible. I could feel its bruise beneath my skin.

My Body Was Telling the Truth

The headaches came next. Not the normal kind - the kind that arrived the moment the skyline appeared, as if my body recognized something my mouth refused to acknowledge.

One morning, sitting in the parking structure, I caught my reflection in the rearview mirror. My smile looked forced. My eyes were tired in a way sleep couldn't touch.

And the truth rose, undeniable:

This wasn't about one woman rearranging my decisions.

This was about me rearranging myself to avoid discomfort.

Silence wasn't keeping the peace - it was costing me my peace.

And the price had become too high.

The Moment I Stopped Making Myself Small

My shift wasn't loud or dramatic. It began as noticing - the kind that keeps tapping you on the shoulder until you finally turn toward it.

I noticed when my body tightened at a false yes.

I noticed when I made myself convenient at my own expense.

I noticed when I softened my truth so someone else could stay steady.

And slowly, I began reclaiming myself:

No more excusing disrespect.

No more shrinking to stay agreeable.

No more treating my discomfort as a reasonable offering for someone else's convenience.

The change was quiet, but the impact was profound.

It was the beginning of choosing myself.

The Becoming Truth

My silence is no longer my offering.
My truth deserves room to breathe.
I refuse to disappear in spaces I've earned the right to stand.

The Becoming Space

Sit gently with these questions:

Where do I silence myself to avoid disappointing someone?

Whose approval am I still auditioning for?

Where do I abandon myself to appear agreeable?

What truth is my body speaking that my mouth keeps denying?

Write without beautifying the truth.

Your Turn to Rise

This week, practice one act of micro-honesty:

"Actually, that doesn't work for me."

"I see it differently."

"I'm not comfortable with that."

Or practice the opposite - refusing to explain yourself when someone demands justification.

Small truth-tellings build the foundation for liberation.

Before You Turn the Page

Silence was my first cage. Breaking it required confronting every cost I had quietly absorbed.

Now we step into the deeper unraveling - the weight women carry without realizing it isn't theirs to hold.

Every becoming has a moment when your hands tremble, your spirit exhales, and you finally whisper, *"I'm done carrying what was never mine."*

Turn the page.

Your freedom is waiting.

CHAPTER THREE

THE WEIGHT I CHOSE TO CARRY

Power Statement

Some burdens don't announce themselves. They slip quietly into your bones until you start believing they're part of who you are.

The Story We Learn Before We Even Know We're Learning

I grew up surrounded by stories no one ever spoke aloud. My family didn't use words like grief, trauma, or fear. Emotions weren't named. Pain wasn't processed. Silence was the culture, and survival was the language we all understood.

My great-grandmother died when my grandmother was fourteen - an age where you should be learning yourself, not raising siblings and shielding them from a father whose anger lived too close to the surface. When her father became angry, he would lock them outside for the day to fend for themselves. My grandmother learned to cook a chicken in the ground and later buried the bones so he wouldn't erupt with more anger upon finding out. That was her normal. That was her protection.

Silence raised her.

And in its own way, silence raised me too.

My father died in a car accident when I was a baby. No one fully explained details of what happened. His absence floated through the house like fog - everywhere and nowhere at once. I carried grief without a story, a wound without a name. By fourteen, the same age my grandmother was forced into adulthood, I began asking questions. Only then did pieces of the truth finally surface.

Silence travels through generations until someone decides it stops here.

When Life Teaches You Strength Before You Have the Language For It

Strength wasn't a choice for me - it was the environment I grew inside of. When emotions have no place to land, a child learns quickly:

Don't ask.

Don't cry.

Don't need.

Just hold it all.

So when I became a teen mom, strength wasn't empowerment - it was instinct. And instead of tenderness, I often met judgment. Eyes followed me through the sanctuary and fellowship hall. Support was shown from some, while scarce from others. Encouragement was minimal. So I did what so many young women do: I stood tall even when I wanted to collapse. I played composed even while learning about motherhood in the midst of feeling alone.

A Small Memory That Still Lives In My Bones

At eighteen, with a baby at home, my cycle started unexpectedly. No pads in the house. Only tampons. I didn't know how to use them, and I didn't feel safe asking my mother. Shame had already taught me to shrink.

So I quietly called the Kaiser nurse line.

A stranger walked me through what my own early young adulthood never taught me.

My voice trembled.

The nurse was kind and gentle.

I hung up, figured it out, and kept going.

That moment didn't break me.

It revealed the loneliness of becoming a woman without some of the guidance I desperately needed.

When Everyone Becomes Your Responsibility And You Becomes No One's

Some children expect help.

Some learn to ask for help.

And some of us are unintentionally taught to be the helper.

I became the strong friend.

The dependable one.

The planner.

The fixer.

People assumed I always "had it" because I always did.

When the pandemic hit and the firm shut down overnight, all eyes turned to me. I organized, solved, held, and carried. Not because I was asked - because it had become my identity.

But no one asked if I was okay.

Not because they didn't care, but because my strength made me invisible.

Competence is often mistaken for capacity.

And that assumption becomes its own kind of weight.

When Tired Isn't Just Tired

My breaking point wasn't dramatic. No collapse. No explosion.

Just a quiet, undeniable truth rising from underneath the life I was holding together.

It was the exhaustion that lives in your spirit, not your body.

The whisper that says:

You cannot keep living like this.

I kept calling burnout "tired."

I kept calling numbness "overthinking."

I kept calling fear "responsibility."

But beneath all of that was the truth my spirit had been trying to say for years:

This is too much.

You are carrying too much.

You are carrying it alone.

The Beliefs That Kept Me Holding What Was Never Mine

Most of the beliefs shaping my life weren't mine - they were inherited patterns dressed up as identity:

You're on your own.
You have to prove yourself.
Asking for help is weakness.
If you don't do it, it won't get done.
Strong women don't need anything.

I didn't even file for child support - a resource meant to help - because somewhere inside, an old voice whispered:

You made this bed. You carry it.

That voice didn't originate with me. It belonged to generations of women conditioned to believe their burdens were destiny.

When A Woman Finally Puts Something Down

I didn't set the weight down because I suddenly felt fearless.
I set it down because my spirit had finally reached its limit.

After a layoff.
After the burnout.
After my body demanded stillness.

I whispered the words I had avoided most of my life:

I need help.

And the world didn't fall apart.

Wanda showed up with generosity.
My ex-husband - still one of my greatest supporters - showed up with steadiness.
Friends respected my boundaries instead of resenting them.

Support met me gently.
And in the quiet that followed, I realized:

The weight wasn't heavy because of what I carried.
It was heavy because I carried it alone.

The Becoming Truth

Strength isn't proven by how much you endure -
Strength is proven by what you release.

Strength looks like:

Asking for help.
Letting people show up.
Resting without guilt.
Saying no without apology.
Breaking generational patterns.
Making room for support.

Some weight is inherited.

Some weight is chosen.

Freedom is intentional.

The Becoming Space

Ask yourself, gently:

What weight am I carrying out of habit, not purpose?

What silence did I inherit that still shapes my strength?

What responsibilities feel familiar but no longer aligned?

Where do I offer myself to others more than I offer myself to me?

What burden - emotional, generational, or practical - can I release now?

You cannot heal what you refuse to name.

And you cannot rise while carrying what was never yours.

Your Turn to Rise

Choose one weight to set down this week.

Maybe it's a role you've outgrown.

Maybe it's a responsibility no one asked you to carry.

Maybe it's a story about strength that no longer matches the woman you're becoming.

Name it.

Write it.

Release it - even in one small way.

Tell someone you need help.

Say no where you once said yes.

Rest where you once over-functioned.

Let your body learn what it feels like to live without that weight - even for a moment.

Before You Turn The Page

The weight you carried wasn't your failure.
It was your conditioning.

But the moment you choose to set it down?
That's the moment your becoming begins.

Turn the page.

*Your freedom is already rising
to meet you.*

CHAPTER FOUR

WHEN THE STRONG ONE BREAKS

Power Statement

My life didn't fall apart in one big moment. It unraveled quietly in the spaces where I kept pretending I was fine.

The Quiet Cracks No One Sees Coming

People imagine breaking as loud - sobbing, screaming, chaos.

But strong women rarely break like that.

We don't shatter.

We erode.

Slowly. Silently. Invisibly.

Breaking can look like answering every text but dodging every call, because a text lets you pretend you're okay without having to sound okay. It looks like staying busy so you never have to sit alone with your own truth. It looks like saying, "I'm fine," with a smile that doesn't quite reach your eyes.

On the outside, I was steady.

Dependable.

The one everyone could count on.

On the inside, tiny fractures were forming - moments where my soul whispered, *I can't keep doing this*, while my mouth said, *I'm okay*.

This is how the strong one breaks: not in a dramatic scene everyone notices, but in the quiet corners no one thinks to check.

The Day My Worth Lost Its Job

The unraveling sharpened the day I lost my job.

On paper, it was employment.

In my spirit, it had become identity.

Work was where my value felt visible.

I was the fixer.

The steady one.

The woman they called when everything fell apart.

So when the title disappeared, I felt myself disappearing with it.

Who was I if no one needed me?

Who was I without deadlines and fires to put out?

Who was I if I wasn't the strong one holding everything together?

The answer I didn't want to face was this:

I had tied my worth to my usefulness.

And when the usefulness went away, the silence inside me was deafening.

Shame, Silence, and the Performance of "I'm Fine"

There is a specific shame that comes when the identity you spent years performing starts to crumble. It whispers:

You should be further than this.
You should've managed life better.
People expected more from you.

So I didn't tell the truth.

I performed it.

I smiled.

I joked about "finally getting a break."

I blamed the job market.

I said I was "resting" while quietly unraveling.

The tears came in private places:

In the car.

In the shower.

In my prayer closet, whispering, *"God, I don't know who I am without work."*

On the outside, I was still high-functioning.

On the inside, nothing about me felt familiar anymore.

When Survival Mode Follows You Into the Breakdown

Survival mode doesn't leave just because you're hurting.
It digs in deeper.

Hold it together.
Don't fall apart.
Don't ask for help.
Figure it out like you always do.

But my body was done cooperating with the old script.

Sleep slipped away.
Tears showed up without warning.
My chest felt heavy, like I was quietly sinking.
Simple decisions suddenly felt like moving furniture in my mind.

I kept trying to power through - but effort wasn't working anymore. My body was telling the truth I kept trying to outthink:

You can't keep carrying this the same way.

I wasn't just breaking down.
I was breaking open - and everything I'd buried started rising to the surface.

Who Still Expected Me to Hold Their World - and Who Held Mine

Breaking seasons clarify relationships.

Some people kept leaning on me the exact same way, not because they were cruel, but because I had never taught them how to support me. I had trained them to see me as the one who "always has it," even when I didn't.

But then there were the unexpected ones.

Certain close friends - checked in regularly, steadying me with a calm presence I didn't know I needed. A few other friends reached out with no agenda, no requests, just softness.

Their presence didn't erase the pain.

But it did soften it.

Breaking showed me two things very clearly:

Who stood with me…

and who had simply been standing on my back.

Learning to Live Without the Performance

After the breaking comes the "after" - and the after is not glamorous.

It looked like slow mornings and quiet days where I didn't recognize my own rhythm. It looked like sitting on the edge of the bed, wondering who I was without a to-do list. It looked like feeling guilty for resting and exposed in stillness.

Space felt threatening.

Stillness felt like failure.

Peace felt like something I hadn't yet earned.

But in that uncomfortable quiet, buried truths started to rise:

I'm exhausted.

I'm overwhelmed.

I feel unsupported.

I'm tired of pretending I'm okay.

I remembered rushing back to work after my twins were born - not because I was ready, but because rest felt like something I had to justify. No one ever taught me how to pause. Life had only taught me how to push.

But breaking pulled me into a different lesson:

Rest is not laziness.

Pausing is not weakness.

Crying is not collapse.

Breaking wasn't the end of me.

Breaking was the beginning of my honest self.

The Becoming Truth

Hold these close:

You are not weak because you break.

You are human.

Breaking is not punishment.

Breaking is interruption - a sacred one.

It is the body saying, "I cannot carry this anymore."

It is the mind saying, "I'm done pretending."

It is the spirit saying, "There is another way to live."

Your breaking isn't a verdict against you.

It's an invitation back to you.

Real strength isn't never bending.
Real strength is finally letting yourself bow.

The Becoming Space

Sit with these questions, gently:

Where have I been pretending I'm okay while quietly collapsing inside?

How much of my worth have I tied to what I do instead of who I am?

Who have I continued to carry that I need to gently set down?

What symptoms - emotional or physical - have I brushed off because they didn't look "dramatic enough"?

If I stopped performing strength, what kind of support would I finally allow myself to receive?

Write without polishing.
Let the truth come out as it is.

Your Turn to Rise

Take one honest pause this week.
Not a shutdown. Not a disappearing act.
A pause.

A moment where you stop performing strength and tell yourself the truth.
It might sound like:

"I'm overwhelmed."
"I need support."

"I can't keep doing this the same way."

One honest pause can redirect an entire breaking season.

Before You Turn the Page

You were never meant to carry everything alone.

Your breaking is not your shame - it's your signal.

On the next page, we step even deeper into what it means to put down the roles, the weight, and the expectations that were never yours to hold in the first place.

The strong one doesn't just break.

The strong one learns a new way to be strong.

Turn the page

when you're ready to let that be you.

CHAPTER FIVE

WHEN "NO" BECOMES THE FIRST STEP HOME

Power Statement

A woman's power isn't found in how much she carries, but in how clearly she decides what she will no longer hold.

The Yes That Slowly Erased Me

For most of my life, I said yes the way other people breathed. Automatically. Instinctively. Without pause.

Yes to favors.

Yes to last-minute requests.

Yes to staying late.

Yes to being available.

Yes to being "the strong one."

I didn't say yes because I wanted to.

I said yes because somewhere deep inside, I believed that no made me difficult, ungrateful, or unworthy of connection.

Survival mode had trained me well:

Say yes so no one is disappointed.

Say yes so no one leaves.

Say yes so peace stays - even if you don't.

Before I learned boundaries, I learned something far more dangerous:
survival through compliance.

I learned it in the shadows - in my mother's shifting moods, in rooms where my feelings had no space to breathe, in the unspoken rule that love required obedience and quiet.

So I became the girl who said yes when her soul whispered no.

And here's what most people misunderstand:

you don't become a people-pleaser because you're weak.

You become one because, at some point, you didn't feel safe.

Every unwanted yes became a slow betrayal of myself.

And that betrayal followed me into adulthood like a shadow that never learned how to rest.

The Lives of a Woman Who Can't Say No

I didn't recognize self-abandonment at first. I mistook it for loyalty. Responsibility. Maturity.

But underneath every instinctive yes was fear:

"They'll be disappointed."
"They'll talk about me."
"They'll leave."
"They'll decide I'm not enough."

So I said yes when I was exhausted.

Yes when my spirit begged to stop.

Yes when my finances said absolutely not.

Yes when all I needed was rest, silence, honesty.

Each yes became resentment layered over fatigue - a quiet ache where boundaries should have lived.

My generosity wasn't generosity.

It was **survival dressed as goodness**.

Eventually, my soul sent the bill.

The Concert Bathroom Breakdown

There was a night I'll never forget. A group of friends planned to attend a concert at the Great Western Forum. They were excited - picking outfits, choosing seats, hyping the moment.

Me?

I was depleted.

What I needed was solitude.

What I said was:

"Yes, I'll go."

I got dressed. Rode along. Smiled like I wanted to be there.

But halfway through the show, something in me snapped - quietly and completely.

I slipped into a bathroom stall, sat on the closed toilet lid, and pretended to be sick.

Not because I was ill -

but because I didn't know how to say the truth:

I don't want to be here.
I don't have it in me.
I'm exhausted.

I remember staring at the stall door, feeling my throat tighten, wishing I knew how to choose myself without apology.

I Ubered home early.

On that ride, I felt two things at once:

Relief.

And shame.

Not shame for leaving -

shame for abandoning myself to get there in the first place.

That night, the version of me who said yes to survive began to unravel.

The Loan That Taught Me The Cost of Self Betrayal

There was another moment - softer, but deeper.

I loaned someone I cared about a large sum of money. Far more than I should have. I told myself it was kindness. I told myself it would be returned.

A year passed.

Barely a payment.

No apology.

No urgency.

The real sting came later, scrolling through social media and happened upon observations of their life at that time.

Trips.

Vacations.

Multiple flights.

International destinations.

And there I was at home, managing bills, tightening my budget... while they lived softly in the space where my boundaries should have been.

They didn't mistreat me.

I underserved myself.

And that truth was heavier than the money.

The First No That Set Me Free

My first intentional no during my growing process came out shaky and soft:

"No... I'm sorry, I can't."

My voice trembled - the old fear rising up, expecting punishment, abandonment, disappointment.

But nothing terrible happened.

No one retaliated.

No one disappeared.

Peace stayed in the room.

That was the moment I learned:

My fear was outdated.

My conditioning was outdated.

The danger was outdated.

But I wasn't.

I had been reacting to threats that no longer existed.

That first no was the first step back home to myself.

When People Show You Who They Are Around Your No

Boundaries don't just protect you - they reveal what you couldn't see before.

When I began saying no, people sorted themselves without effort.

The Acceptors

They said, "Okay." No guilt. No drama. No side comments.

The Adjusters

Surprised at first, but willing to shift. They stayed - respectfully.

The Resistors

The sighs. The guilt-tripping. The subtle punishments. The entitlement. The sudden distance. These were the ones who had been accustomed to and benefited most from my lack of boundaries.

Their reactions taught me something sacred:

My no was never the problem.

Their expectations were.

No isn't rejection.

No isn't punishment.

No isn't a wall - **it's a doorway back to yourself.**

The Becoming Truth

You deserve a life where:

Your needs matter.

Your voice is honored.

Your yes is aligned.

Your no is respected.

You don't shrink for comfort.

You don't sacrifice yourself for connection.

Your no is not selfish.

Your no is not mean.

Your no is sacred -

because it's honest and it's yours.

The Becoming Space

Sit with these questions gently:

Where have I been saying yes out of fear instead of desire?

Which version of me is still trying to earn love through compliance?

Who am I afraid to disappoint, and why?

Where do I need rest, but keep offering labor?

What was the last moment I betrayed myself to keep a connection alive?

What would my life feel like if I trusted myself enough to say no?

Let honesty rise without judgment.

Your Turn to Rise

Practice one boundary this week - just one.

Say no without explaining.

Say yes only when your whole body agrees.

Cancel something you committed to out of guilt.

Leave a text unanswered until you have emotional space.

Protect one moment of peace like it's sacred - because it is.

Boundaries aren't punishment.

They are self-respect in action.

Before You Turn the Page

When a woman stops performing for worth, she begins to hear her own voice again.

No loosens what once held you captive -

but loosening is only the beginning.

The next chapter is where the unraveling meets your becoming -the in-between space where the old self slips away and the new one hasn't fully arrived.

Turn the page.

The messy middle is waiting for you.

CHAPTER SIX

THE MESSY MIDDLE:
THE PART OF BECOMING THAT NO
ONE WARNED YOU ABOUT

Power Statement

Every woman wants to rise…but no one tells you that rising always begins with unraveling.

The Part You Can't Pretty Your Way Through

There comes a moment in every woman's becoming - a quiet, terrifying, holy moment - when the life she built out of survival starts to come undone in her own hands.

Not dramatically.

Not loudly.

Not with mascara streaks and slammed doors.

The real unraveling feels like waking up and realizing something inside you has shifted, and you no longer recognize yourself in the life you're living.

It's sitting in your car after another long day, hands on the steering wheel, forehead pressed against it, whispering, *I can't keep doing this.*

It's walking through your own home and feeling like a visitor in the life you created.

It's feeling the strength you used as currency suddenly lose its value, while the pieces you've carried for decades begin to slip through your fingers.

No one warns you about this part.

Because becoming doesn't just break you down.

Becoming breaks you open.

When the Life You Built Starts Talking Back

At first, I thought I was just tired.

There is tired.

And then there is soul-tired.

My soul-tired moment came the day I lost the job that had been holding up my identity. The job where competence became my personality. The job where strength was my native language.

On paper, it was a layoff.

In my spirit, something much deeper was collapsing.

When I went back to the building because I'd forgotten something and found my badge deactivated, I stood there in front of the scanner - hand frozen, heart pounding - feeling something in me shut down and wake up at the same time.

I was losing employment, yes.

But what I was really losing was the version of myself I only knew through labor.

I had always been the strong one. The dependable one. The woman who "figures it out." Then, one quiet afternoon, I couldn't figure anything out - not even myself.

I didn't know who I was without accomplishment.

Without a title.

Without motion.

Without a crisis to manage and a fire to put out.

That silence was the beginning of my messy middle.

When Survival Mode Stops Working

It took years for me to name what I had been living in for decades: **survival mode.**

Not a season.

Not a buzzword.

A way of being so familiar I mistook it for my personality.

It looked like:

Being strong because no one else could be.

Saying yes because no felt dangerous.

Carrying what was never mine.

Feeling guilty for needing help.

Smiling with a tight chest while whispering, *I'm fine* on repeat.

Survival mode isn't loud.

It's quiet obedience. Quiet fear. Quiet loneliness.

You don't realize you've been living in it until your body refuses to stay there.

For me, the refusal happened softly, in places no one saw.

In the closet where I prayed, cried, and whispered truths I wasn't ready to say out loud.

In the car, where the steering wheel knew more of my tears than my pillow ever did.

In the shower, water running over my face as I asked God, *Is this really what life is supposed to feel like?*

That was the unraveling.

The holy undoing.

The beginning of becoming.

The Emotional Closet You Avoid Until You Can't

The messy middle feels like cleaning out a closet you've been stuffing for forty years.

You pull out one thing, and ten others tumble out with it:

A grief you never named.

A childhood wound you outgrew but never healed.

Friendships you've outgrown.

Relationships you tolerated.

Weight you carried that never belonged to you.

Masks you wore because silence felt safer.

Before long, you're sitting on the floor, surrounded by pieces of a life you no longer fit inside.

I saw roles piled all around me:

The strong one.

The dependable one.

The self-sacrificing one.

The woman who never asks for help.

The woman who trades rest for responsibility.

The woman who confuses being needed with being valued.

Looking at it all was overwhelming. Part of me wanted to shove it all back in - even the parts that hurt.

Because chaos can feel familiar.

And familiarity can feel safe, even when it's slowly suffocating you.

The Fear No One Talks About

People think fear is about danger.

But one of the deepest fears is this:

Who am I without the version of myself I've always been?

I was afraid of being seen.

Afraid of being soft.

Afraid of needing help.

Afraid of releasing the identity I fought so hard to build.

I knew how to be a strong woman.

I had no idea how to be a free one.

So yes - some days I snapped.

Some days I overcorrected.

Some days I defended myself with more force than the moment required because I was learning how to use a voice I'd spent a lifetime silencing.

Healing isn't neat or linear.

It's layered - like peeling off armor you welded to your own spirit. Under every layer you remove, another truth is waiting, asking, *Now can we be honest?*

Rest: The First Revolution

When everything fell apart, I called it failure.

What I didn't realize was that my body had finally refused to cooperate with my survival mode. I was being pushed - lovingly, firmly - into rest.

Not sitting down while your mind keeps spinning.

Not crashing from exhaustion.

Not hiding from people under the covers.

I'm talking about **holy rest** - the kind your soul demands when you've ignored it too long.

In that rest, I learned something that changed me:

I did not suddenly vanish.

My world did not collapse.

The people who truly loved me didn't vanish when I wasn't "useful."

They still saw me.

They still loved me.

Not for what I carried - but for who I was when I finally put things down.

I learned that the people meant for you don't stay because you hold their world together.

They stay when you finally allow your own world to breathe.

The Becoming Truth

Hold these close:

You cannot rise while clinging to the woman you had to be to survive.

You have to release her - not because she was wrong, but because she was built for a war you're no longer fighting.

Your messy middle is not a sign of failure.

It's the evidence that the old you is shedding.

You are not breaking down.

You are breaking open.

The life that no longer fits you is not a punishment.

It is a signal.

You are not losing yourself.

You are finally meeting her.

The Becoming Space

Take a breath. Let your shoulders drop. This is your space to be honest.

Ask yourself:

What am I still carrying that feels too heavy for who I am now?

Where in my life do I feel like a visitor instead of a resident?

What roles have I outgrown but keep performing out of habit?

What emotions have I been stuffing into the "closet" of my life, hoping they'll disappear?

If I stopped pretending I was fine, what truth would finally come out of my mouth?

Do not edit your answers. Your honesty is not dangerous.

It is sacred.

Your Turn to Rise

Give yourself permission to do one small, radical thing this week:

Name one role you're tired of playing.

Write it down.

Then write a single sentence that begins with:

"I am allowed to stop…"

You might write:

"I am allowed to stop being the one who fixes everything."

"I am allowed to stop pretending I'm not hurt."

"I am allowed to stop carrying responsibilities that do not belong to me."

Then choose one tiny, tangible act that honors that statement:

Rest instead of volunteering.

Say no instead of automatically saying yes.

Let a tear fall instead of swallowing it.

Small shifts in the messy middle become the foundation of the woman you're becoming.

Before You Turn the Page

The messy middle is not where your story ends.

It is where your story becomes honest.

You are not failing.

You are loosening what no longer fits.

Every becoming has a season where everything feels undone, unfamiliar, uncertain - and that is exactly where your new life starts to breathe.

Turn the page.

Next, you'll learn what happens when
you loosen your grip and let your
life begin to flow.

CHAPTER SEVEN

LEARNING TO LIVE IN FLOW

Power Statement

There comes a moment in every woman's becoming when she realizes she has been holding life in a fist. Her healing begins the second she finally opens her hand.

Where the Grip Begins

Control is often misunderstood.

It dresses up as confidence, hides behind structure, and wears responsibility like a crown. But underneath, control is usually fear - fear that if you stop holding everything together, everything will fall apart.

When you grow up gripping for safety, letting go can feel like losing your balance. But in truth, it's the first time you are standing on solid ground.

For years, I wasn't controlling life out of arrogance.

I was controlling life out of instinct.

Control was my childhood armor - my quiet way of keeping myself safe in a world where truth wasn't always believed and fairness wasn't always practiced.

I didn't choose control.

Control chose me.

Where Control Was Born

My grip started long before I knew to call it control.

As a girl, I lived in an apartment complex where the landlord watched the children from her window like a lookout post. Her grandchildren caused chaos, but when trouble surfaced, her voice always found me.

It didn't matter who started it.

It mattered who she decided was responsible.

I learned quickly that fairness had loopholes, truth had limits, and speaking up didn't guarantee safety.

My shoulders tightened.

My voice shrank.

My instincts chose silence.

Not because I wanted to hide, but because hiding felt safer than being blamed.

I recall when years later, the pattern resurfaced with a family member who shielded her daughter's harmful behavior. Anytime I tried to offer gentle honesty, it was met with defensiveness, dismissal, or deflection.

The message was clear:

Don't challenge.

Don't disrupt.

Don't be honest if honesty creates discomfort.

Those echoes layered themselves into a quiet, powerful belief:

Silence keeps the peace.

Responsibility keeps you safe.

Control keeps the world steady.

Letting go?

That felt like betrayal.

The First Unclenching

Letting go did not arrive as a revelation. It began as a softening in my chest before I had language for it - a quiet loosening, a gentle release, a shift so subtle I almost missed it.

Most of my life, I held things tightly:

People.

Outcomes.

Expectations.

Reactions.

Peacekeeping.

Responsibility.

I gripped not because I wanted to, but because I didn't trust what would happen if I didn't. When you've spent a lifetime managing emotional weather - anticipating storms, adjusting to moods, offering stability - you start believing your grip is the only thing holding everyone together.

But healing whispered something truer:

You don't have to hold everything.

You were never meant to.

And when I finally started listening, my fingers began to open.

The Day My Voice Held Steady

My breakthrough didn't happen in therapy. It didn't arrive in a journal.

It showed up on a regular workday.

A supervisor raised her voice in a high-stress moment. In an old version of me, I would have shrunk, softened, apologized, or over-explained to make it easier for her - not for me.

But this time, my voice rose before fear could silence it.

Calm.

Clear.

Steady.

I explained exactly what I was doing. I named the impact of the yelling. I spoke truth without trembling, without hostility, and without abandoning myself to maintain harmony.

She apologized.

She adjusted.

She acknowledged me.

And in that small, ordinary moment, something extraordinary happened inside me.

The grip cracked.

Light rushed in.

That day taught me that using your voice is not the opposite of flow.

Using your voice is part of the flow.

The Moment Flow Found Me

Flow didn't arrive wrapped in ease. It arrived as alignment.

After a layoff, I stepped into a business-management role while quietly pursuing a longtime dream: working for an airline.

When the airline invited me to train in Florida, my first instinct was to say no. It didn't feel "responsible." I almost closed the door before I even touched the handle.

But something in me whispered, *Ask anyway.*

So I did.

They said yes.

No resistance.

No tension.

No chaos.

Just doors opening where I had once learned to expect walls.

I trained in Florida. I worked remotely. I balanced both roles with a grace that did not match the math on paper.

For the first time in my life, I wasn't pushing.

I wasn't forcing.

I wasn't micromanaging every detail or bracing for the worst.

I was being carried.

That is the quiet miracle of flow - when life starts moving with you instead of against you.

The Day Laughter Returned

Letting go has a physical sensation, but it isn't always tears or trembling.

Sometimes, it sounds like laughter.

Real laughter.

Loud laughter.

Belly laughter.

The kind that rises out of your body before your mind can overthink it. The kind I hadn't heard from myself in some time.

It slipped out in conversations.

It echoed in my home.

It surprised me at work.

I would hear myself and think, *Oh... there she is.*

My laughter came back first.

Flow followed right behind.

It was the sound of a nervous system finally exhaling.

The sound of a life that had unclenched because I had unclenched inside it.

The Becoming Truth

You cannot enter flow with clenched fists.

Alignment cannot reach a woman who is still gripping her past.

Grace cannot fill hands that are still holding fear.

Letting go is not passive.

It is the most active kind of trust.

It is the sacred exhale after decades of emotional breath-holding.

It is the beginning of becoming the woman you were always meant to be.

The Becoming Space

Sit gently with these questions:

Where am I holding on out of fear instead of intention?

What am I trying to manage that is costing me my peace?

Which version of me feels too tight for who I'm becoming?

What might open if I loosened my grip just a little?

Where is life trying to flow, but I keep bracing?

Let the answers rise without judgment.

Flow begins with honesty.

Your Turn to Rise

Release one small thing today.

Not everything.

Not all at once.

Just one thing.

Say no without apologizing.

Let someone help you with something you always do alone.

Stop rehearsing a truth you're afraid to speak.

Leave a text unanswered until your spirit is steady.

Trust the timing of something you cannot force.

Every loosening is liberation.

Every release is a rise.

Before You Turn the Page

Letting go is not the end of your strength.

It is the beginning of your ease, your clarity, your alignment.

When a woman opens her hand, she becomes available to the life that has been waiting to unfold.

Flow is not somewhere "out there."

Flow is what happens when you stop gripping long enough to be carried.

Turn the page.

Next, we step into what it means to trust
the timing of your becoming -
even when it doesn't look anything like
you thought it would.

CHAPTER EIGHT

THE SPACE BETWEEN: LETTING GO BEFORE THE NEW ARRIVES

Power Statement

Your life changes the moment urgency stops feeling responsible and starts feeling like a prison - because that's the doorway where ease finally enters.

When Exhaustion Becomes Identity

There is a moment in a woman's life when exhaustion stops being a feeling and quietly becomes her identity.

Not because she is careless.

Not because she is failing.

But because she has been holding the entire architecture of her world together for so long, fatigue starts to feel like her personality.

You stop even questioning it.

You normalize the tight chest.

You normalize the shallow breathing.

You normalize the overbooked days, the rushed mornings, the guilt that rises every time rest whispers your name.

You start calling it "life," while your body tells another truth entirely:

You were not created to survive your own life.

You were created to live it.

When Your Body Speaks Before You Do

My body knew I needed ease long before I ever said the word.

It knew in the jump of my heart at every notification.

It knew in the way I rearranged myself around other people's needs.

It knew in the way I braced for the day instead of breathing into it.

For years, I believed that tension meant responsibility. If I felt tight, pressured, and overwhelmed, I told myself I was being diligent.

But there came a morning when that belief finally cracked.

The Morning That Reintroduced Me to Myself

I had a remote workday - a rare moment of built-in spaciousness.

I told myself, *I'll walk before I log in.*

I wanted fresh air. Sunlight. Movement. Just a little room to breathe.

But the old voice rose up like a reflex:

You don't have time.

Just log in.

You can walk tomorrow.

Handle your responsibilities first.

That voice had been running the show for decades.

But that morning, something soft and steady inside me whispered back:

No. We're walking.

So I listened.

I stepped outside expecting twenty minutes.

Twenty became forty.

Forty became sixty.

And an hour became a slow, unhurried stroll through a neighborhood I had only ever rushed through.

No bracing.

No clock-watching.

No guilt.

Just breath.

Just presence.

Just ease.

For the first time in a long time, I wasn't performing urgency.

I was choosing myself.

The Little Dog With the Big Message

Halfway through my walk, a neighbor approached with a tiny dog on a leash.

This little dog kept drifting toward me, tugging with all its might, circling back every few steps as if it were drawn to the quiet softness rising in me.

I laughed - not a polite, measured laugh, but the kind that shakes something loose inside your ribs.

In that simple moment, it felt like a wink from God.

When you choose yourself, life responds.

When you soften, joy notices.

When you stop gripping, flow finally has room to enter.

That little dog became a reminder:

Joy had been trying to reach me.

I had just been too tense, too rushed, too responsible to receive it.

When You Stop Rushing, Nothing Falls Apart

I walked back home.

I showered.

I logged in to work - later than usual.

And nothing happened.

No emergencies.

No crises.

No disasters.

Everything was fine.

And that quiet *fine* shook me more than any meltdown could have, because my whole life had been built on an unspoken contract:

If you loosen your grip, everything will collapse.

But the truth was simpler and much kinder:

My world was never held up by my tension.

It was being held up by grace.

The Cost of Living on Urgency

That morning, I finally called it what it was:

I wasn't driven by responsibility.

I was driven by urgency.

Urgency I inherited from women who never had the luxury of rest.

Urgency rewarded by workplaces that glorify burnout.

Urgency that made me feel important, useful, irreplaceable.

And when urgency becomes your identity:

Ease feels reckless.

Rest feels indulgent.

Joy feels suspicious.

Stillness feels like failure.

But the moment I stopped performing urgency, I realized something I had been too busy to see:

Letting go didn't make me fall apart.

Letting go made me whole.

The space between the old life and the new one wasn't empty.

It was where my nervous system finally exhaled.

The Becoming Truth

You cannot grip fear and receive joy at the same time.

You cannot worship exhaustion and expect peace to stay.

You cannot perform survival while praying for alignment.

There is a version of you waiting on the other side of your rush.

She is softer.

She is freer.

She is wiser.

And she is done waiting for permission.

The Becoming Space

Take a breath.

Place your hand on your heart.

Let your body speak first.

Ask gently:

Where am I rushing out of habit rather than need?

What am I gripping because I'm afraid life won't be okay without me?

Where is ease trying to enter, but I keep blocking the doorway?

What would shift if I gave myself one guilt-free hour?

What truth is my body whispering that my mind keeps overriding?

Let your answers rise - unedited, unfiltered, unjudged.

Your honesty is not irresponsible.

It's the beginning of your freedom.

Your Turn to Rise

If you journal, take these to the page. If you don't, just let them roll around in your mind as you move through your week:

What small act of ease can I choose this week?

What urgency have I been mistaking for importance?

Where am I performing strength instead of living truth?

How can I let myself breathe without bracing?

Where is life trying to meet me, but I keep rushing past?

Then choose one tiny act of rebellion against urgency:

Take the slower route.

Sit in the sun for ten minutes.

Let an email wait.

Walk without your phone.

Rest without explaining why.

Ease is not a luxury.

Ease is a lifeline.

Before You Turn the Page

Ease is not the opposite of strength.

It is the next evolution of it.

In this space between who you were and who you are becoming, you are learning to live without the constant emergency siren of urgency.

Next, we step into a deeper truth so many women live silently:

When belonging comes with conditions, you lose yourself piece by piece.

Chapter Nine begins there...

...in the rooms where you contorted yourself to stay, and the woman you meet when you finally refuse to do it anymore.

CHAPTER NINE

WHEN BELONGING COMES WITH CONDITIONS

Power Statement

I do not have to perform to be worthy.

I do not have to earn love to be loved.

I belong - fully, deeply, and without condition.

When "Being Good" Becomes the Price of Belonging

There is a specific ache that forms in a woman who has spent her whole life trying to be *good*.

Not whole.

Not honest.

Just... good.

Good enough to be accepted.

Good enough to silence judgment.

Good enough to walk into a room without fearing what people will whisper.

When "good" becomes your identity, belonging stops being a birthright and becomes a contract. You don't feel loved - you feel managed. You don't feel seen - you feel monitored. And deep down you learn to fear that one wrong move could cost you everything.

Conditional belonging is not belonging at all.

It is approval dressed as acceptance - and it has an expiration date.

The Day My Worth Was Put on Trial

I was eighteen. Pregnant. Terrified. Trying to understand how a moment of humanity had turned me into a morality lesson.

My church - the place that raised me, the place I trusted - called a meeting.

Not to comfort me.

Not to guide me.

Not to pray over my shaking heart.

They gathered to determine my punishment.

I sat outside while adults filled the front of the sanctuary for their Board Meeting, deciding what to strip from me - my duties, my visibility, my place of belonging.

I could attend.

But I could no longer serve.

I could sit in the pews.

But not stand on the platform.

People hugged me at service and some whispered about me at potluck. Some threw me a baby shower in public while some threw stones in private. Smiles mixed with judgment. Sympathy mixed with shame.

It was punishment dressed as righteousness.

Holiness wrapped in optics.

And the wound wasn't just the discipline - it was the realization that my worth had conditions.

When the Pattern Repeated With My Daughter

Years later, my oldest became pregnant in college. Twenty-two. Away from home. And some of the same community that once celebrated her suddenly vocalized their tone.

Judgment where there should have been compassion.

Silence where there should have been covering.

Someone who grew up around her posted online comments rooted not in truth but in assumption. Meanwhile, another woman in the extended family - married, older, "acceptable" - announced her pregnancy and was met with congratulations.

The difference in treatment was unmistakable.

Watching my daughter walk through the same wound I once carried cracked something ancient inside me.

The echo was loud:

Some of us are allowed to be human.

Others are made into warnings.

The Truth About Hypocrisy

Age gave me clarity I didn't have at eighteen.

I began to see that some of the adults who punished me were quietly wrestling with their own contradictions. The pastor who once guided me gently eventually faced circumstances that mirrored what the church condemned in me.

No judgment.

No shade.

Just truth:

Everyone carries something.

But only some of us are punished for it, whether publicly or energetically.

Belonging in those spaces was never about holiness.

It was about image, control, and respectability politics.

I had been transformed from a member into a message.

What Conditional Belonging Taught Me About Myself

Early on, I learned that acceptance came with rules.

Visibility came with fine print.

Worth came with conditions.

So I performed.

I spoke "correctly."

I dressed "appropriately."

I excelled professionally.

I overextended emotionally.

I said yes when everything in me whispered no.

I became the polished, reliable, careful one - because deep down I believed what the church taught me without ever saying:

You must earn love.

You must behave your way into belonging.

You must never disappoint the room.

But conditional belonging is never real belonging.

It is applause with strings attached.

It is approval on a timer.

And even when people praised me, I still felt outside of myself - because I wasn't being loved. I was being managed.

When I Finally Stopped Performing for Worth

The shift didn't arrive as a rebellion - it arrived as a quiet decision.

I began stepping back from spaces that required performance.

Stopping the constant explaining.

Saying no without offering a sermon.

Letting calls go unanswered when they only came with demands.

Choosing alignment over obligation.

Choosing peace over perception.

And somewhere in that gentle unraveling, I discovered something life-altering:

I belong to me first.

When a woman belongs to herself, the need for conditional rooms dissolves. Not instantly. Not neatly. But steadily, like someone turning on a light inside her chest.

The more I honored my truth, the less willing I became to sit in spaces where my worth was up for debate.

The Becoming Truth

I am not here to prove my worth.
I am here to live it.
My value is not up for a vote.
My humanity is not negotiable.
I will not pay for belonging with pieces of myself.

The Becoming Space

Breathe.

Let your truth rise gently.

Where have you been performing for approval instead of living in alignment?

What rooms require you to shrink, edit, or silence yourself to stay included?

When did you first learn that belonging came with conditions?

What did that moment teach you about *them* - and about you?

What would unconditional belonging feel like in your breath, your shoulders, your body?

Who are you when you're not pleasing, perfecting, or performing?

Your honesty is not rebellion.

Your honesty is return.

Your Turn to Rise

This week, practice belonging to yourself in one small, sacred way:

Speak without rehearsing.

Rest without guilt.

Say no without apologizing.

Wear something that feels like *you*.

Tell the truth without shrinking it.

Show up exactly as you are - not as you think they prefer.

One act of authenticity becomes a lifetime of freedom.

Before You Turn the Page

When a woman stops performing for worth, she comes home to herself.

But coming home means releasing the weight you carried to earn a place in rooms that were never yours.

Chapter Ten asks the question your soul has whispered for years:

What if you finally put down everything you were never meant to carry?

Turn the page -

the release begins there.

CHAPTER TEN

WHEN YOU FINALLY PUT DOWN WHAT WAS NEVER YOURS

Power Statement

The moment I stopped performing for love was the moment I finally remembered who I was.

When Performance Quietly Becomes Identity

There comes a point when you've been performing so long that the performance starts performing *you*.

You keep showing up the way you always have - helpful, capable, overprepared, over-responsible, impossibly strong. At first it looks like excellence. Then the doing becomes proving. And the proving quietly becomes identity.

For years, I believed my worth lived in my work. In being the fixer. The steady hand. The one who answered every email, solved every problem, carried every crisis.

I didn't just *do* the work.

I *became* the work.

But the truth about performing for worth is simple:

There is no finish line.

There is no arrival.

There is no rest.

Just the next thing to prove.

When the Stage Disappears

When I lost my job at the law firm, I didn't just lose income. I lost the stage where my worth had learned how to breathe. The title disappeared. The urgency vanished. The never-ending list of people to save went silent.

And suddenly, the only person left in the room was me - a woman I had never slowed down long enough to really know.

I cried in the shower.

I cried in my prayer closet.

I sat on the floor and whispered, *"Who am I now?"*

I thought I was grieving employment.

I was actually grieving a version of myself that believed she had to earn every inch of her existence.

When the Body Tells the Truth First

I tried to keep pushing. Applying. Interviewing. Pretending I was "fine." But my body refused.

Anxiety.

Overstimulation.

Fatigue that sleep couldn't touch.

A fog that sat between me and everything I was trying to force.

When the doctor said, "stress-related disability," I felt two things at the same time:

Panic - because rest had always felt like failure.

Permission - because someone finally gave language to the breaking I had been minimizing for years.

Disability wasn't just time off.

It was a mirror.

And staring back at me was a woman who had never been allowed to stop moving long enough to meet herself.

When You Stop Proving and Start Becoming

Stillness became my teacher.

Not the kind of stillness where you hide under blankets scrolling your phone, but the kind where you can finally hear your own life.

I started walking again - slowly, without tracking steps or turning it into a goal. I let myself rest without apologizing for it. I listened to my own thoughts without bracing for impact. I breathed on purpose.

In that quiet, new questions rose up:

What if nothing is wrong with me?

What if something was wrong with the way I was taught to survive?

Piece by piece, my spirit started coming home.

The Day a Stranger Bought My Coffee

A few months into that season, I was at an airport with coworkers - laughing, grabbing coffee, simply *being*, not impressing anyone.

A young man stepped up to the counter and said to the cashier, "No, I've got hers."

No flirting.

No agenda.

No strange energy.

He paid, smiled, and walked away.

It was such a small moment, but something in me cracked open.

For the first time, I realized I wasn't bracing for the catch. I wasn't trying to earn the kindness or read between the lines. I just received it.

This wasn't the woman who hustled for validation.

This was the woman who had been quietly unclenching - letting God hold what she could no longer pretend to carry.

Worth shifts your energy long before it shifts your circumstances.

When Strangers Start Noticing the Real You

After that, I started noticing a pattern.

Men on escalators offering warm, passing smiles, simply being kind.

Coworkers complimenting my joy instead of my output.

Strangers holding doors, making space, extending small kindnesses without expecting anything back.

The world hadn't suddenly changed.

I had.

Kindness had probably been there all along - but I finally had room inside to let it land.

My laughter returned - big, loud, unfiltered.

My presence softened.

My spirit felt lighter.

I wasn't performing anymore.

I was becoming.

And people responded to the woman I was finally meeting, too.

When Your Children Start Mirroring Your Becoming

Then came the moment that melted me.

My youngest daughter, in her twenties, started saying something that makes me grin every time:

"Mom, I'm staying home this weekend… I'm gonna **use my rent**."

Use. My. Rent.

She meant she was going to enjoy the space she pays for. Rest in it. Be still in it. Let it hold her.

In that simple sentence, I heard a generational shift:

She was choosing rest at twenty.

Choosing peace at twenty.

Choosing herself at twenty.

The practices I didn't honor until my fifties... she was already claiming as normal.

My healing had become her blueprint.

My worth had become her inheritance.

My self-honoring had become her example.

Rest is not laziness.

Rest is leadership.

The Becoming Truth

Your worth is not something you earn.

Your value is not something you hustle for.

You do not have to collapse to be cared for.

You do not have to perform to belong.

You are already enough - without effort, without proving, without the mask.

When you finally put down what was never yours to carry, your soul remembers who she has always been.

The Becoming Space

Ask yourself gently:

Where have I tied my worth to my work?

Who am I when I'm not performing, fixing, or proving?

Where have I been bracing instead of receiving?

What responsibilities have become identity instead of choice?

What truth is trying to land in me, but I keep rushing past it?

Your answers are not inconveniences.

They are revelations.

Your Turn to Rise

Choose one act of worthiness this week - one that requires no performance at all:

Rest without guilt.

Say no without a speech.

Allow help without apology.

Tell the truth without shrinking it.

Receive kindness without suspicion.

One honest moment of receiving can begin to heal years of overgiving.

Before You Turn the Page

When a woman stops proving her worth, she doesn't become less.

She becomes herself.

And in the next chapter, we step deeper into what rises in the quiet after performance ends - the truth about identity, alignment, and becoming the woman you were always meant to be.

What you release reveals you.

Now that your hands are open, something new is ready to land.

Turn the page.

Your becoming continues.

CHAPTER ELEVEN

THE COCOON: WHEN LIFE PRESSES PAUSE SO YOU CAN BEGIN AGAIN

Power Statement

Sometimes life won't let you continue as the woman you were - because the woman you're becoming needs more than your old identity can hold.

When Life Pulled Me Out of My Own Hustle

My cocoon didn't begin with clarity. It began with loss - the kind that strips you down to truth before you're ready.

The layoff...

The overwhelm...

The slow cracking of an identity built on doing, fixing, rescuing, managing, performing.

For years, motion was my medicine. Productivity was my hiding place. I didn't see how deeply I had rooted my worth in being useful - or how much survival mode had become home.

And then suddenly, everything stopped.

For the first time in decades, life whispered:

"Sit down. Be still. Something in you needs to breathe."

I mistook it for punishment.

But it was preparation.

The Identity I Didn't Know I Needed to Release

Before the cocoon, I was the reliable one.

The provider.

The doer.

The strong one who carried what no one saw and asked for nothing in return.

But when my rhythm changed, when responsibilities loosened, when the world no longer needed me at full speed, an uncomfortable truth rose:

I didn't know who I was without the hustle.

I started reevaluating everything - not out of scarcity, but out of awakening. Closets, spending habits, old routines, even the things I bought to make exhaustion feel pretty. The pruning wasn't about money. It was about identity.

The cocoon stripped away a belief I had worshipped for years:

"If I'm not producing, I'm not valuable."

The cocoon came to dismantle that lie.

The Mirror My Daughter Held Up to Me

During that season, I poured myself into a project with someone who wasn't matching my effort. I carried the planning, the execution - the entire weight - then felt resentful when they didn't.

One afternoon, tired and frustrated, I vented to my oldest daughter. She listened, then said something that sliced through decades of over-functioning:

"Mom... you can't keep being mad that people aren't you."

Whew.

It was a sentence and a rescue. I suddenly saw how often I had sprinted ahead of people, doing for them what they never asked for, then calling it disappointment when they didn't respond like I would.

The cocoon doesn't shame you - it confronts you with the truth required for freedom.

The Stillness That Reintroduced Me to Myself

Once the dust settled, something unfamiliar wrapped around me:

Stillness.

My kids were more independent.

My schedule loosened.

My mornings slowed.

My evenings quieted.

I found myself reading in my closet, praying in silence, taking slow walks just because my spirit wanted air. I cooked simply because it brought joy. I napped in the middle of the day without guilt. I spent real time helping my family with joy. I learned what my body needed instead of demanding more from it.

And in the quiet, I heard:

"See? Nothing falls apart when you stop holding up the world."

Instead... something inside you begins to rise.

The Becoming Space

Breathe. Let these questions meet you gently:

Where has life paused me so I could finally see myself?

Where am I grieving identities that kept me alive but never aligned?

Where have I mistaken exhaustion for purpose?

What am I afraid will happen if I stop rescuing everyone?

What expectations am I carrying that were never mine to hold?

Let the truths surface softly.

The Becoming Truth

I honor the season I'm in.

I am safe in stillness.

I release identities that once protected me but now restrict me.

I trust the pauses life gives me.

I surrender the need to be everything for everyone.

I choose alignment over autopilot.

Stillness is not the absence of progress.

Stillness is where a new direction is born.

Your Turn to Rise

Choose one thing you've been holding out of habit or fear - and let it go this week.

One role.

One expectation.

One obligation that drains more than it develops.

Release it.

Then watch what peace grows in the space it leaves behind.

Before You Turn the Page

Your cocoon season is not collapse.

It is clearing.

Reordering.

A divine interruption designed to return you to yourself.

Because once you've surrendered…

Once you've softened…

Once life has stripped you down to truth…

You begin to rise with a strength that doesn't force - it flows.

And in the next chapter, we step into that gentle strength - the soft power that emerges when survival mode finally loosens its grip.

Stillness has done its work.

Now your becoming takes shape. When you're ready, turn the page.

CHAPTER TWELVE

THE SUPERPOWER OF SOFTNESS: TURNING TENDERNESS INTO TRUTH

Power Statement

Softness didn't make me smaller. Softness made me sovereign. I didn't rise because life got easier - I rose because I stopped confusing hardness with strength.

When Survival Teaches You to Fear Yourself

There is a kind of womanhood you don't learn - you inherit.

Women who were raised to endure rather than feel.

Women who kept the family stable, even when it was breaking inside.

Women who carried storms with a straight face.

We weren't taught softness.

We were taught survival.

So I learned to treat tenderness like a liability. I believed emotions made me vulnerable. I believed gentleness made me a target. I believed hardness was the only safe option.

The truth was simpler than I wanted to admit:

I didn't lack softness.

I was afraid of it.

When My Reflection Asked for Mercy

The day softness found me wasn't pretty.

No candles.

No journal.

No curated moment of peace.

Just me, sitting on the floor of my closet, finally quiet enough to hear the truth I had outrun for years.

What surfaced wasn't loud pain - it was buried pain:

The shame I never addressed.

The resentment I swallowed.

The guilt I carried like currency.

The self-betrayal I disguised as loyalty.

The decisions I punished myself for long after they were over.

And in that stillness, my spirit whispered words I didn't even know I needed:

You don't need punishment. You need mercy.

That sentence cracked my armor.

Softness didn't tiptoe in - it poured.

The Self-Forgiveness That Rebuilt Me

No one tells you that self-forgiveness is fierce.

It doesn't arrive as a gentle pat on the back. It walks in like a mirror and says, "Look. Really look."

As I began forgiving myself, I finally saw:

The years I abandoned myself to keep the peace.

The relationships I outgrew long before I left.

The friendships where I over-functioned until resentment moved in.

The moments I accepted crumbs and called it loyalty.

The times I chose attachment over alignment.

Forgiveness wasn't relief.

Forgiveness was a homecoming.

It didn't erase the past - it released the version of me who kept paying for it.

The Conversation Where Softness Became Sovereignty

There was a situation where, in the past, I would have swallowed my discomfort to protect someone else - said nothing, made excuses, carried the tension alone.

Old me would have called it "being understanding."

Really, it was self-abandonment.

Soft me handled it differently.

I approached the conversation with calm clarity - not force, not fury. I named the truth without overexplaining it. I honored my feelings without attacking theirs. I spoke from self-respect, not fear.

And for the first time, I didn't spiral afterward.

I didn't rehearse different endings in my head.

I didn't soften my truth in my mind to justify their behavior.

I felt steady.

I felt rooted.

I felt sovereign.

Softness had taught me how to honor myself *and* keep my heart open.

Parenting With Softness - Healing the Next Generation

For years, I parented from fear.

Fear of what might happen.

Fear shaped by old wounds.

Fear of the world, the streets, the cars, the what-ifs.

I was loving, but intense.

Protective, but anxious.

Present, but heavy.

Then one day, my daughter said quietly, "Mom… you don't have to be so hard on yourself."

Her words landed deeper than she knew.

I realized that my children weren't just learning from what I said to them. They were learning from how I spoke to myself.

Softness didn't weaken my parenting.

Softness made it more connected, more honest, more healing.

I still set boundaries. I still protected. But the edge softened. The pressure loosened. The air between us became safer - not because I controlled more, but because I carried myself with more compassion.

Sensitivity Is a Superpower

I used to be called "too sensitive."

Too emotional.

Too affected.

So I tried to harden myself. I tried to feel less, need less, care less.

But after years of softening, I finally understood:

My sensitivity was never a weakness.

My sensitivity was the compass.

It was my intuition.

My discernment.

My spiritual accuracy.

Sensitivity didn't make me fragile.

Sensitivity made me truthful.

It let me feel when something was off before it became obvious. It nudged me toward alignment when my mind wanted to negotiate. It warned me when my spirit started shrinking.

My tears were not the problem.

Ignoring what they were trying to say was.

The Woman Softness Built

Softness redefined my strength.

Today, softness looks like:

Speaking without overexplaining.

Saying no without guilt.

Letting people feel their feelings without rescuing them.

Releasing relationships that shrink me.

Honoring what nurtures me instead of tolerating what drains me.

Choosing alignment over attachment.

Letting myself feel deeply without apology.

Softness didn't make me less powerful.

Softness made me whole.

The Becoming Space

Slow down. Breathe. Answer honestly:

Where have I been too harsh with myself?

Where am I punishing myself for decisions I've already outgrown?

Where have I mistaken sensitivity for weakness?

Where am I shrinking so someone else can stay comfortable?

Where am I choosing attachment when alignment is long gone?

Where do I need to extend mercy to myself?

Where is softness trying to heal me, but I keep resisting?

Let your answers reveal what your spirit is ready to release.

The Becoming Truth

I forgive myself fully and without hesitation.

My sensitivity is sacred.

My softness is my wisdom.

I honor my needs without apology.

I can be gentle and still be powerful.

My boundaries are holy.

My intuition is trustworthy.

Tenderness is truth.

Your Turn to Rise

Start small - softness grows through repetition.

Write yourself the apology you needed years ago.

Replace one criticism with one comfort each day.

Speak one truth you've avoided.

Set one clean boundary without overexplaining it.

Trust your intuition the first time - not the twelfth.

Softness is a practice.

Softness is a power.

Softness is a return.

Before You Turn the Page

Softness didn't make me fragile.

Softness made me ready.

Ready for surrender.

Ready for alignment.

Ready for the life I was always meant to live.

Because once you stop fighting yourself, you finally have the capacity to let life unfold *with* you instead of around you.

In the next chapter, we step into what softness prepared me to see clearly:

that you are not behind - you are being prepared, redirected, and aligned with a timing that has always been bigger than your own plans.

When you're ready, turn the page.

Softness has opened the door.

Timing is waiting on the other side.

CHAPTER THIRTEEN

TRUSTING THE TIMING OF MY BECOMING

Power Statement

I am not late. I am right on time. When I stopped rushing my life, my life finally started meeting me where I was.

When You Think You're Behind… But You're Actually Being Positioned

There is a specific kind of ache that comes from believing you've missed your moment.

It's the ache of scrolling through pictures of marriages, vacations, new homes, promotions, and milestones, thinking,

Did I fall behind?

Did I miss the deadline on my own becoming?

I carried that ache for a while - a quiet panic in my spirit. A whisper that everyone else had "figured life out" while I was still trying to remember where I put my own map.

Behind in love.

Behind in healing.

Behind in finances.

Behind in purpose.

But slowly - gently - a new truth rose inside me like a sunrise I didn't realize was happening:

You are never behind when your life is aligning you.

Timing isn't a race.

Timing is an invitation.

The Seasons That Lied to Me About Being Behind

There were seasons where it felt like life was taunting me.

Everyone else seemed to be arriving.

I felt like I was still packing my bags.

I watched women settle into long marriages while mine had ended. I watched women purchase dream homes while I was rebuilding my financial life from scratch. I convinced myself certain men were "the one" simply because I was tired of waiting.

As I approached my fifties, I remember thinking, *How did I get here without the things I thought I'd have by now?*

But, baby… life wasn't punishing me.

Life was positioning me.

Those years weren't evidence that I was late. They were evidence that my story was being written differently.

The Man I Walked Away From - and the Woman I Walked Back Toward

There was a man I genuinely cared for.

He was attentive, funny, warm.

A good father.

A good human.

A comfort in a world that can feel sharp.

But over time, something in my spirit grew louder than the comfort. Truth was rising.

We lived in two different emotional climates.

He survived through distraction.

I healed through stillness.

He needed noise to settle his nerves.

I needed quiet to hear my soul.

He wanted more of my time.

I needed more of my own.

He wasn't a villain. He was simply not aligned with my becoming.

Old me would've stayed.

Would've bent myself into whatever shape made him comfortable.

Would've dimmed my evolution so he could avoid his.

But the woman I am now?

She does not shrink for love.

She does not abandon her peace for companionship.

She does not betray her becoming to keep someone company.

So one ordinary evening, with my spirit steady and my voice clear, I told him the truth:

"I care for you. I respect you. But we are not aligned - and I cannot keep choosing someone else at the cost of myself."

There was no chaos.

No screaming.

No dramatic scene.

Just clarity.

Walking away didn't break me.

Staying and ignoring my truth would have.

That moment taught me something sacred:

Not every ending is a loss. Some endings are liberation.

Not every separation is rejection. Some separations are redirection.

Not every man is meant to stay. Some arrive to show you who you refuse to stop becoming.

Timing wasn't denying me love.

Timing was aligning me with myself.

The Job That Didn't Happen - and the Life That Did

There was a prestigious legal position - shiny on a résumé, impressive in conversation - and I was the top candidate.

Every interview flowed. Every meeting felt promising. It looked like the perfect next step. Then came the background check. An erroneous flag on the credit report. A technicality I didn't even know existed.

The door didn't just close.

It slammed.

Locked.

Bolted itself shut.

I was devastated. Embarrassed. Quietly ashamed. I told myself I had failed. I told myself I'd missed my moment. I told myself my timing had run out.

But had I gotten that job, I never would have said yes to the airline opportunity - the one that became a doorway into joy, community, travel, healing, and unexpected purpose. The job that let me breathe again. Write again. Thrive again.

Sometimes we think the blessing is the door that opens.

But often, the blessing is the door that refuses to.

The Financial Reset That Rewired My Pace

For years, I was used to big responsibilities and big checks. Then life shifted - layoffs, disability, transitions - and my income changed.

It was humbling. Sometimes humiliating. I had to ask for help when I was used to being the helper. I had to face the truth about how often I used spending to soothe stress and look "together."

That season didn't just reset my bank account.

It reset my rhythm.

I moved slower.

I paid attention.

I noticed how often I tried to buy the feeling of "enough."

Losing income didn't mean I was slipping. It pulled me off the hamster wheel and brought me back to myself. I started greeting mornings instead of surviving them. I started being present instead of just productive.

I wasn't falling behind.

I was being recalibrated.

I Was Never Failing. I Was Being Redirected.

When I finally stopped moving long enough to breathe, everything I had buried began rising - old choices, old patterns, old places where I abandoned myself, old habits of giving others more power than I gave myself.

For the first time, I didn't run from the mirror.

I stayed.

I looked.

I grieved.

I forgave.

Forgiveness didn't slow me down.

Forgiveness aligned me.

The urgency faded.

The panic quieted.

The comparison loosened its grip.

The more compassion I gave myself, the less I believed the lie of "behind."

Trusting My Life Instead of Rushing It

Over time, something softer and wiser took root.

I stopped dating people who interrupted my peace.

I stopped forcing relationships that weren't aligned.

I stopped believing marriage had to happen "by now."

I stopped shaming my financial story.

I stopped rushing seasons that needed rest, not movement.

I started trusting the pauses.

I started trusting the detours.

I started trusting the doors that didn't open.

Every reroute held wisdom my future self would need.

Every delay carried protection I couldn't see yet.

Every shift was positioning.

I was never behind.

I was being prepared.

The Becoming Truth

Speak these gently. Let them sink into your bones:

I am the right woman in the right season.

I am aligned, not delayed.

Nothing meant for me is ever late.

I am being prepared, not punished.

My life is not behind - my life is becoming.

I release comparison and embrace my own path.

My delays are divine redirections.

The Becoming Space

Take a breath. Let your shoulders drop. Let truth land where it needs to.

Ask yourself:

Where have I been telling myself I'm "behind"?

Whose timeline am I secretly measuring myself against?

What closed door still feels like failure instead of protection?

Where am I rushing because I'm afraid of being still?

What season am I resisting instead of trusting?

Your life is not running late.

Your life is running deep.

And depth takes time.

Your Turn to Rise

This week, let patience be your quiet practice.

Identify one place you've been calling yourself "behind."

Write it down - plainly, without judgment.

Then ask:

Whose story made me think I'm late?

What might this season be protecting or preparing me for?

Take one small action that agrees with trust instead of panic:

A slow walk instead of a frantic scroll.

A prayer instead of a spiral.

A journal page instead of a comparison session.

A chosen rest instead of a forced rush.

Release urgency.

Let your life breathe.

Let yourself breathe.

Before You Turn the Page

Trusting the timing of your life is one thing.

Walking boldly as the woman that timing has prepared you to be is another.

In the next chapter, we step into that power - the courage to rise as the healed, aligned, grounded version of yourself. The woman who no longer rushes, forces, or fears her path… because she finally understands that every step brought her here.

And here is exactly where she's meant to rise.

The final rise begins now.

CHAPTER FOURTEEN

I MAY STILL BE BECOMING… BUT I WILL NEVER ABANDON MYSELF AGAIN

Power Statement

Becoming didn't save me - choosing myself did.

Becoming isn't an endpoint. Becoming is a devotion to evolving without apology.

When Chasing "Enough" Becomes a Lifelong Sprint

For most of my life, I was sprinting toward a finish line that didn't exist.

If I loved harder…

If I gave more…

If I performed better…

If I endured longer…

If I shrank smaller…

Maybe then I'd finally feel worthy of rest.

Maybe then I'd feel lovable.

Maybe then I'd stop apologizing for my existence.

But one day, truth met my exhaustion and said, *"Baby, step off this track."*

There is no arrival point for worthiness.

Worthiness is your birthright.

Becoming is not a competition.

Becoming is a deep inhale - a turning inward, a returning home.

The Day I Stopped Apologizing for My Own Life

My resurrection wasn't loud.

It didn't come with applause or permission.

It came the moment I told the truth - to myself, about myself.

I had spent years granting everyone else the right to be fully human, while denying myself the same grace.

I apologized for resting.

For feeling.

For naming my needs.

For wanting peace.

For changing.

For using my voice.

But becoming requires a rebellion - a holy insurrection against self-abandonment.

The first time I used my **unedited voice**, something ancient rose inside me.

My intuition stood up.

My spirit stretched her back.

My identity rearranged itself.

And I saw myself clearly:

I was never "too much."

I was never "too sensitive."

I was never "too emotional."

I was never "too honest."

I was simply becoming.

Becoming Is a Lifelong Unfolding

We were conditioned to believe life must follow a script to be valid - love by a certain age, success by a certain age, healing on a clock.

But who wrote that script?

And why were we following it like gospel?

Your becoming does not honor deadlines.

Your becoming honors truth.

I once believed I was "behind" because my story didn't mirror the women around me.

But the truth arrived gently:

You are never late to your own evolution.

Had I forced myself into someone else's timeline,

I would have missed the woman I am right now:

A woman with clarity.

A woman with boundaries.

A woman with self-trust.

A woman who knows her worth in the dark, not just in the light.

I Am No Longer Who I Was - And I'm Not Done Becoming Who I Am

So much has fallen away…

And so much has risen in its place.

I no longer silence my needs.

I no longer negotiate my boundaries.

I no longer shrink to be chosen.

I no longer carry what was never mine.

I no longer contort myself for acceptance.

I no longer trade my peace to keep the room comfortable.

Becoming required release.

Release created room.

And in that room… I found myself.

The Becoming Truth

You are allowed to evolve without permission.

You are allowed to release stories that suffocate you.

You are allowed to outgrow who you were told to be.

You are allowed to choose peace over performance.

You are allowed to rewrite every chapter of your life.

You are allowed to rise - boldly, beautifully, endlessly.

The Becoming Space

Hand on your heart. Deep breath.

Ask yourself:

Where have I abandoned myself in the name of being loved?

Where have I been loyal to patterns instead of purpose?

What version of me is hurting me, yet I keep protecting her?

What truth have I swallowed to avoid upsetting someone?

What would my life look like if I chose myself the way I choose others?

Who could I become if I stopped apologizing for my evolution?

Your next level isn't waiting on the world.

Your next level is waiting on your permission.

Your Turn to Rise

Identify one place you've abandoned yourself - reclaim it today.

Release one old version - thank her for surviving.

Set one clean boundary - softly, firmly.

Do one bold act of self-belief - the kind that even surprises you.

Then declare these aloud:

I am not behind.

I am right on time.

I honor my becoming, even when it feels uncomfortable.

I release the need to earn love or prove my worth.

I owe no one an explanation for my evolution.

I forgive myself fully.

I trust myself deeply.

I rise without apology.

I am becoming the woman God always saw in me.

The Final Becoming

You get to rewrite your story.

You get to love yourself wildly.

You get to outgrow versions of yourself that once felt safe.

You get to honor your voice.

You get to build a new lineage.

You get to be the first woman in your family to become emotionally free.

You get to rise without explaining why.

You get to walk away from survival.

You get to live rooted in truth, not performance.

You get to be soft and strong.

You get to be powerful and gentle.

You get to be whole and still becoming.

You get to be you - fully, boldly, beautifully you.

I may still be becoming…

but now I release the need to earn love, prove my worth, or explain my becoming to anyone.

Before You Turn the Page

The book may end here -

but you do not.

You are stepping into a dimension where your softness is strength,

your truth is liberation,

your voice is your compass,

and your becoming is endless.

You are not waiting on permission.

You are not waiting on timing.

You are not waiting on validation.

You have arrived.

And the world - *your* world -

is about to meet the woman you will never abandon again.

Because you, my dear…

are still becoming.

And the becoming is endless.

IF I COULD TELL HER ONE THING

A Sacred Manifesto for the Woman Becoming

If I could tell her one thing-

the one truth meant for the quiet corners where she hides-

it would be this:

You are not running out of time.

You are running into yourself.

I would tell her that the world lied to her about what it means to be worthy, lovable, successful, or "on track."

That the timeline she disciplines herself with never belonged to her.

It belonged to someone else's fear, someone else's expectations, someone else's imagination of her life.

She is not late - **she is layered.**

And the layers make her extraordinary.

I would take her shame gently in my hands and whisper,

"This was never yours to carry."

I would remind her that the softness she buried to survive was her superpower…

and the voice she silenced to keep the peace was always the key to her liberation.

I would tell her she never had to earn love.

She is love.

She never had to chase worth.

She is worthy.

I would tell her that her "mistakes" were rehearsals for the wisdom she walks in now,

her "setbacks" were divine reroutes,

and the places where she felt abandoned were altars where she learned to choose herself first.

I would tell her to rise.

To take up space.

To stop dimming her light because someone else preferred shadows.

I would tell her she is allowed to become a woman her past self would barely recognize-

soft and powerful, humble and unstoppable, gentle and fierce.

And if I could tell her one final thing, it would be this:

Choosing yourself is not the end of your becoming.

It is the beginning.

Because the moment she decides she will never abandon herself again,

the entire world rearranges to meet her.

She doesn't need perfection.

She doesn't need certainty.

She doesn't need fearlessness.

She just has to be herself-

fully, boldly, beautifully herself.

She is already becoming the woman she once prayed she'd have the courage to be.

And she is only getting started.

ON THE JOURNEY TO
BECOMING YOU...

May you rise with grace for who you were,

and reverence for who you're becoming.

May your voice return to you-clear, unshaken, whole.

May your softness guide you.

May your boundaries protect you.

May your truth free you.

May your becoming unfold in divine rhythm -

never rushed, never forced, always aligned.

May you release what is heavy.

May you embrace what is holy.

May you trust what is true.

May you honor yourself with the same devotion you have so freely given to others.

And may you never again -

from this day forward -

abandon yourself.

You are becoming.

You are rising.

You are home.

ACKNOWLEDGMENTS

There are seasons in life when you rise because of your own strength...

and seasons when you rise because of the people God placed around you.

To my children

You were my first purpose, my greatest teachers, and the mirrors that revealed the woman I was becoming.

Thank you for standing with me through every shift, every transition, every unraveling, and every resurrection.

You are my heart's most sacred work.

To my family and close friends

Your support, your laughter, your patience, and your presence carried me through the hardest chapters and celebrated me through the sweetest ones.

Thank you for seeing me even when I didn't yet know how to see myself.

To the women who have shared their own experiences with me

Your vulnerability gave me permission.

Your wisdom steadied me.

Your resilience reminded me that I was never walking alone.

To every reader holding this book

You are the reason I wrote this.

I may never know your name, but I wrote these pages like I knew your heart.

May this book be your mirror, your guide, your companion, and your sacred permission to return to yourself.

And most importantly... to God

For every closed door that was protection.

For every reroute that was redirection.

For every quiet moment where You whispered me back to myself.

This book exists because You held me together long before I understood I was breaking open.

ABOUT THE AUTHOR

Shawnta Auston is a writer, speaker, creative visionary, and transformational guide for women ready to rise - from survival into selfhood. A mother since eighteen, a grandmother, a corporate professional, and a lifelong student of becoming, she has built a life anchored in faith, truth, courage, and emotional evolution.

After decades of suppressing her own voice and carrying identities that were never hers to hold, Shawnta embraced her personal reinvention in her fifties - choosing softness, alignment, and self-honoring over performance, perfectionism, and survival. Her work is rooted in a powerful truth: women are not meant to remain who they were. They are meant to evolve into who they were always called to be.

Known for her genuine heart, honesty, soulful storytelling, and warm, wise, and often witty presence, Shawnta inspires women of all ages to reclaim their voice, shed old identities, trust divine timing, and embrace becoming as a lifelong devotion. Her writing blends spiritual insight with lived experience, guiding women back to themselves with compassion, clarity, and courage.

She resides in Southern California, where she continues to write, speak, laugh loudly, love deeply, and walk in the freedom she once prayed for - living proof that reinvention is always possible, and that it's never too late to become the woman you were created to be.